"My first thought upon my Journible arriving was wow! I plan on purchasing at least one of these for each of my girls. I would like them to have a copy of handwritten Scripture from me. Possibly in the future they will want to purchase their own copies and use them personally. The 17:18 Series would also be good to use in your homeschooling. They are great for copy work and handwriting practice. Plus you will be using the Word of God with your children. The Word of God never returns void."

—Melissa, mother from Trenton, Florida

"I really enjoy this resource because it causes me to slow down and to think about what I'm reading and writing, to meditate on aspects of the Word that I otherwise might just skim. It's true that I don't have time to read as big a chunk of Proverbs every day that I usually do, but what time I do have is rich with new insight and meaning."

—Jasmine, homeschool student and daughter of Voddie and Bridget Baucham, Spring, Texas

"The Journible I am currently using covers the books of James, 1 and 2 Peter, 1–3 John, and Jude. I have spent the last two weeks slowly making my way through James, and it has opened my eyes to the Scriptures like never before. Not only am I reading the Scripture, but I am writing it, meditating on it, answering thought-provoking questions, and reflecting on how my life should change to reflect what the Scriptures teach."

—Jeremy, pastor from Jacksonville, Florida

The 17:18 Series

Journible® through
Ruth

Joel R. Beeke and Rob Wynalda

This book belongs to:

_____

Given by: _____

Date: _____

REFORMATION
HERITAGE BOOKS

Published by
Reformation Heritage Books
2965 Leonard St. NE
Grand Rapids, MI 49525
616-977-0889
email: orders@heritagebooks.org
website: www.heritagebooks.org

ISBN 978-1-60178-752-1

Cover Design: Bethany Sanderson and Steve Coy
Journible® Design: Rob Wynalda

Why the 17:18 series?

In Deuteronomy 17, Moses is leaving final instructions concerning the future of Israel. As a prophet of God, Moses foretells of when Israel will place a king over the nation (v. 14). In verses 16 & 17, he lists items that the king could not do as king. In verse 18, he transitions to what he should do as king.

The king is commanded not to simply acquire a copy of the law (the entire book of Deuteronomy) from the "scroll publishing house," but to handwrite his own copy of the law. The purpose of such a copy written by his own hand was so that:
  * he would read it
  * he would learn to fear the Lord
  * he would obey the commands of God
  * his heart would not become proud
  * he would not turn to the right or the left from following the law (Prov. 4:27)
  * also, his sons would serve in the kingdom after him (Deut. 17:19, 20).

Thirty-four hundred years later, educators are "discovering" that students who physically write out their notes by hand have a much greater retention rate than those who simply hear or visually read the information. Apparently, God knew this to be true for the kings of Israel also.

From such understanding came the conception of this series of books.

Have a great time writing and learning the Word of God,

Rob Wynalda
Romans 1:16

5

The Purpose of the Journible®

Engagement:

The Journible® is a profoundly simple attempt to aid a person's ability to engage the Word of God by slowing down the process of simply reading the text. The book is organized so that the "scribe" can slowly and thoughtfully engage the text while leaving plenty of room to write comments and questions about the text (Deuteronomy 17:18; Psalm 119; 2 Timothy 3:16, 17).

Legacy:

Journibles® provide a legacy to pass on from one generation to the next. The Journible® creates an opportunity for one generation to communicate in writing to the next generation their insights and personal applications of the text (Deuteronomy 6).

How to use this book

This book is organized so that the scribe (you) will handwrite your very own copy of Ruth. You will be writing the text of the Bible only on the right-hand page of the book. This should make for easier writing and also allows ample space on the left page of your open text to write your own notes and comments. From time to time a question or word will be lightly printed on the left page; these questions are to aid in further study, but should not interfere with your own notes and comments. This means that you are encouraged not only to write your own "copy" of the Bible, but also to write your own notes concerning the text.

Yes, we are setting aside our mass-produced Gutenberg Bibles and attempting to get back to the simple handwritten copy of the text.

(1) During what period did Ruth enter redemptive history? What was Israel's spiritual condition at this time (see Judg. 2:11–13)?

(1–2) What was the reason for these Israelites living in Moab?

(3–5) Apart from the sorrow of bereavement, why was it tragic in ancient times for a woman to lose her husband and sons?

(4) What is the potential danger of marrying Moabite women (see Deut. 7:1–3)?

(5) If you had experienced the trials that Naomi does here, how would you be tempted to perceive God?

(6) What is Naomi's basis for going back to her hometown? How is her returning a picture of repentance?

1

2

3

4

5

6

(8-9) What does Naomi's statement toward her daughters-in-law indicate about her character? Why would she send them away?

(11) Why would Naomi mention her womb?

7

8

9

10

11

12

Notes

(13) How does Naomi view God's relation to her?
Is her view of God correct?

(15—17) What did Ruth commit to Naomi? What is the
religious significance of this commitment?

13

14

15

16

17

18

Notes

(19) Bethlehem means "house of bread." Why is its name ironic in this story?

(20) What do the names Naomi and Mara mean?

(21) How does the Lord providentially govern the bitter and painful events in the lives of His people?

(22) Why does the narrator continue emphasizing that Ruth is a Moabite?

19

20

21

22

Notes

(1) What does this verse tell us about Boaz?

(2) What provisions had God made in the law for the poor and widowed to gather food (see Lev. 19:9–10; Deut. 24:19)?

(3) Why would the narrator say that Ruth just happened to stumble upon the field of Boaz? Is this a random event?

(4) In the midst of a godless age, what does Boaz's greeting indicate about his spiritual condition?

1

2

3

4

5

6

(9) How was Boaz's command for the men not to touch Ruth rooted in God's law (see Deut. 22:25–27).

(10) Why is Ruth so overwhelmed by the grace Boaz shows to her? How is this similar to the response Christians should have to the grace of Christ?

7

8

9

10

11

(12) What is the imagery of God used by Boaz here (see Ps. 36:7; 91:4)?

(14—16) How does Boaz's kindness toward Ruth exceed the statutes of the law?

(17) How much is an ephah of barley? Approximately how long would this have lasted Ruth and Naomi?

12

13

14

15

16

17

Notes

(20) Who extends the kindness referred to by Naomi—God or Boaz?

18

19

20

21

22

Notes

(23) How long was a typical harvest time?

23

Notes

(1) What does Naomi mean by "rest" (or "security") here (see Ruth 1:8; 4:13)?

(2) What was the purpose of a threshing floor? How does John the Baptist use it as a metaphor (see Matt. 3:12)?

(4) Why would Naomi instruct Ruth to lie down at Boaz's feet?

1

2

3

4

5

6

Notes

(9) How does the imagery here harken back to Boaz's prayer in Ruth 2:12?

(10) How was Ruth showing kindness to Boaz?

(12) In this verse, Boaz takes on the role of a kinsman-redeemer. What would it entail for Boaz to redeem Ruth?

7

8

9

10

11

12

(14) Why would Boaz not want it to be known that Ruth had visited the threshing floor?

(17) How does Boaz function as God's means of blessing to Ruth and Naomi?

13

14

15

16

17

Notes

8

(1) In ancient Israel, what was the significance of the town gate?

(2) Why were the elders invited to sit down with Boaz and the close relative (also called a kinsman and a redeemer)? (See Deuteronomy 21:19; 22:15; 25:7.)

(3—4) Why would Boaz and the close relative care if Naomi is selling land (see Lev. 25:25)?

(5—6) Why did the close relative decide not to redeem Naomi's estate?

1

2

3

4

5

(8) What was the significance of removing one sandal?

(8-10) In what way(s) does Boaz point to Christ?

6

7

8

9

10

(11) How was Ruth used to build up the house of Israel?
What is the significance of God accomplishing this through
a Moabite?

(13) Who enables Ruth to become pregnant? Why is this
significant?

(14—17) How did the Lord reverse Naomi's bitter and
empty situation, which she lamented in Ruth 1:20—21?

1

2

3

4

5

6

Notes

(18—22) What is the messianic significance of this closing genealogy (see Isa. 11:10; Rom. 1:3; Rev. 22:16)?

17

18

19

20

21

22

Notes

Notes

Notes

Notes

Journibles™ have the look and feel of a classic journal, with a black hard cover, gold foil title, and ribbon bookmark. Just like in this Psalm 119 booklet, right-hand pages feature chapters and verse numbers, which are conveniently spaced according to the length of each verse. Left-hand pages are left blank for your notes and comments on the text. Scattered throughout in light print are questions to guide your thoughts as you study that particular portion of Scripture. As you copy the Scriptures and engage the text in a deeper, more thoughtful way, you will find yourself retaining the truths of God's Word.

While Journibles are special tools that will enhance your own personal study of God's Word, here are some other great ways to use them:

- *A lasting legacy for your family*—Include your own special notes about certain passages of Scripture. Your immediate family—and generations to come—will benefit from your insights!

- *Youth ministry*—Use Bible study time to write out Scripture passages, and then discuss them—or assign a passage outside of study time, and discuss it and students' notes when you come together.

- *Small groups*—Leaders assign a passage to write, and then group members come together and discuss their notes.

- *Congregational study*—Pastors challenge church members to write out the text for sermons in advance on right-hand pages and take notes on left-hand pages during the sermon.

- *Discipleship tool*—Spiritually mature believers can use Journibles to shepherd young believers toward spiritual growth.

- *Educational resource*—Good tool for copy work, handwriting practice, reading, and Bible study curriculum.

- *A great gift*—for graduation, birthday, or Christmas. Write your own special note of encouragement inside before you give it away!